Questio
Views

By

Levi Ames

Questionable Views

Author: Levi Ames

First Published in 2023

ISBN 978-1-915796-05-9 (Paperback)
978-1-915796-06-6 (E-Book)

Book cover design and Book layout by:
White Magic Studios
www.whitemagicstudios.co.uk

Published by:
Maple Publishers
Fairbourne Drive, Atterbury,
Milton Keynes,
MK10 9RG, UK
www.maplepublishers.com

A CIP catalogue record for this title is available from the British Library.

Be a friend with an ear to lend

Objective

Well I just want to start out by saying that the purpose of this book of poems to me is to hopefully resonate with people and make them feel less isolated in their thoughts , these are my thoughts and feelings laid out bare and take from it what you will hopefully to see even though you can feel like you're as low as a snake in a wagon wheel rut it doesn't have to define you - which personally I think people have a tendency to do nowadays forgetting the fact that at the crux of it all we're all human wanting a world of peace for us and ours and defining ourselves by one thing can only cause division ..... that might sound simplistic it might sound trite but hey if it evokes a reaction it's all good open discussions about these subjects is what's needed without people being shut down, it appears to me the slowest thing to evolve on this planet is mans ability to be open and objective and our personal pasts and heritage need to be acknowledged but so as not to mar the future , so I hope anyone who takes the time to read this book might get something positive from my Blunt Prose Poetry.

Whats in Your Head

Clocking in and clocking out
This can't be what it's all about
Wasted talent
And undiscovered skills
The boredom's dealt with
Drinking beer and popping pills
So there's another withdrawal
From the brain cell bank
Tick along in an existence
Not worth a wank

Work and Politics

The Class Ceiling

What's going on with a system that only makes the wealthiest more wealthy
It's not your fault
If you weren't born in Chelsea
Social mobility issues for generations
Deprived teens with low expectations
Work yourself out of poverty they say
Without any help coming your way
University fees
They bring you to your knees
A privileged background
That'll help with degrees
They'll keep you down with their work ethic
Get you into a job earning minimum wage
Make you feel pathetic
They don't need you educated
Or having self esteem

That's not part of their scheme
That's not at the top of their list
Their only need is for you to exist
They all went to Public school
They were simply born to rule
And use a language that isn't spoken
Rules ignored by them are never broken
Could they live on the living wage
A thought that should fill the working class with rage
Bring them down from their ivory towers
Have them working zero contract hours
The toil and sweat of working classes
Should land the aristocracy on their asses.

The Populist Shame

Trump & Johnson are not worthy
When extreme inequality and depletion of resources collide
Self preservation your fate will decide
Comprehension of what life beholds
When society as we know it folds
A nightmare transcending reality
The movie watched the game played and the book read
It won't be the same as your avatar falling down dead
With Populist Politicians leading the world
With their right wing dreams and flags unfurled
They're already looking after number one
While people sleep in their cars
They're sending rockets to Mars
Inequality and oppression
Holding hostage on the precipice of a great depression.

Disgrace

Disgrace of the human race
People pushed from pillar to post
People whom no one wants to host
People displaced from their respected roles
Facing persecution from security patrols
Many perils faced on route
Hopes for a better future
The refugees pursuit
Where would one be
In that position
If it were thee?

Western Waste

You have clothes in wardrobes
And drawers you don't need.
For a fashion trend you feed
Clothes you'll never wear
The ones you do , are thrown
Rather than repair
Try and find your passion
In other than fast fashion
Designer brands on African sand
Capitalism consumerism ruins the land
Turnover of Ts
Piled higher than the trees
Beachfronts littered with clothes
Where it'll end no one knows

Fight the Power

Shall I tell you a story
About the working class Tory
Instead of keeping this Island afloat
They decided to sell out their given vote
Falling for lies of a Etonian fool
From a world so detached it's cruel
Filled with thoughts of others to blame
Fed to them in the populist game
Being hostile to the weak
That's a Tory technique
Promises of Hospitals
That don't get built
It doesn't bother them
They have no sense of guilt

Furlough

Furlough was ok
Benefits came their way
Because it was them in need
And they had mouths to feed
Yet for people with nothing
They see it as greed
That's the logic
Of those filled with lies
And Tory vitriolic

News to Confuse

I'm just an old guy
With some political views
I don't understand
What's going on in the news
4.3 billion lost in fraud
Crisis going on while ministers holiday abroad
Stealth tax on graduates
120,000 soldiers on the Ukrainian border
Declining birth rates
I see the return of the toilet roll hoarder
Brexit and covid and Johnson's mess
A nonchalant prime minister
He couldn't care less
Billions spent on phone apps that don't work
Millions more given to Etonian friends business
The man's just a jerk

Young people listen hear
The voice you have
You should hold dear
They want you to look down
On people who have nothing
While they steal your hard earned taxes
Distracting you with their huffing and puffing
WAKE THE FUCK UP!

Life and Death

You'll know when they're gone

Menopause

It isn't a weakness

Death benefits

Exit Left

Anti

Even though you're gone

I

Introspection

What is Love

Helping Heal

You'll Know When They're Gone

One by one
They disappear
The ones you've loved
The ones who care
The one who thought you were a God
Returned to the soil like unwanted sod
I could have got you stuffed
And kept you around
Instead, we put you into the ground
I would have had you there to see
Sleeping in the corner,
That would comfort me
The short strong man
With Iron like fists,
Oh my Dad you really are missed.

Menopause

The menopause has fucked you up
Lack of sleep and hot sweats
Have filled your cup
You need to know I'm there
Whatever when or where
If you lose your mind your looks or your hair
My love won't fade
I'll always be there

It isn't A Weakness

I struggle with my sanity
And not to utter profanity
Trying my best to please
Brings me to my knees
Because with being kind
Some will mess with my mind
Your mental health
That's down to yourself
That's the reality
Of your own sanity
People that post
Often turn Ghost
It's just lip Service
God preserve us.

Death Benefits

It's the natural loss adjuster
Gives you back stuff
Life with them couldn't muster
It might be wearing slacks
Instead of a skirt
It might Simply be chatting
Or being a flirt
Whatever you can't condemn
As it does not change
Their love of them.

Exit Left

Suicide isn't painless
I carry it in my back pocket
As if it were a lucky charm
Or a picture in a locket
Just in case you see
I need a way to be free
You would only understand
If you were dealt my hand

Anti

She wasn't my cup of tea
The Aunt that was given to me
She wasn't the Aunt I would have chosen
She's cold and selfish
With a heart that's frozen
She would summon you
And expect you there at the drop of a hat
No thought for you
You just had to, that was that
Loyalty of family
And doing the right thing
Oh the heartache
That can bring

Even Though You're Gone

The restless soul
The bigger part
The unslept whole
What the fuck can I do
What can I do
To gain approval of you
Sentenced to a lifetime
Of self hate and guilt
A prisoner of yours
In this netherworld
You built.

I

I don't visit your grave
Because you're not there
You are in my head
And everywhere
Drills spanner's and grinders
Are everyday reminders
Like the good deeds you did
Set an example for this kid
Not perfect by any means
But your loss , your loss
That's ripped me to the seams

Introspection

What's your objective
What's your goal
Have you ever thought
Delved into your soul
What's the rush
But don't waste your time
Plenty to do
But what's it achieve
Do you wonder
Do you believe
Or do you ignore
Is it instinct
Or do you abhor
Are you wearing blinkers
Of ignorance and hate
Take a hold of your mind
Sanctify yourself
And regenerate .

What is Love

Sometimes it's a reflex
Often quite complex
It can come out of the blue
And get the better of you
Some will get excited
But not if it's unrequited
You'll not know what to do
When it's thrown back at you

Helping Heal

Cliches and platitudes are so easy to use
And they in themselves are pragmatism for the blues
When mystified for something to say
Sometimes it's best to keep those thoughts at bay
Just to listen and say nothing can be an aid in itself
Empathy you might say is the word of the day

The Children

Re•a•son
They'll bring ....
Ineffectual Intellectual
The evil that Mums do
I seen him regular
If you want a positive outcome
Fostering thoughts

Re•a•son

My boys a man
That's so hard to comprehend
When I think to myself
He came out of my penis end
A strapping young man
Who makes us so proud
I want to tell everyone
And shout it out loud
The world can be tough
Wanting him safe
And knowing he's loved is enough.

They'll Bring…

Joy to your life
Or except that's what you hope
Instead it could be soiling
That can't be erased with soap
Head lice bed bugs and verrucas
And some come with attitude
That's more than just rude
Expectations beyond what they've seen
They want everything you've got
And to go everywhere you've been
Damage beyond repair
From parents that just don't care
You do your best to make them feel cared for
Despite the fact they'll call you a wanker a cunt or a whore
These are facts not just some assumptions
They'll fuck up your life with their epic disruptions

Don't get me wrong
It's not the Kid's fault
It's their formative years
They only know what they're taught
And their Parents possibly had the same
Experiencing things they shouldn't To THEIR parents shame
And like a twisted merry go round
So it goes on staining their fate
Until Social workers decide to take earlier action to eradicate
Eradicate the cycle of abuse
Surely that's what they are there for to conduce.

Ineffectual Intellectual

They say the west brought it on
These deprecating fools
That would follow Putins rules
Upset with actions that were defensive
Not actions that are offensive
A world watched on as a wall was formed
Out of Tanks and military
Many just kids uniformed
And just as unaware
Of what was to be performed
In a Sunflower loving Nation
Despot degradation
Phones ring in abandoned bags in the station
Sign of the INVASION of a peaceful Nation
Sign of the war that Putin took to Ukraine

One man's greed causing so much pain

One sided peace talks are futile

A message saying for our Children on an exploded missile

A missile that killed more than 50 refugees.

The Evil that Mum's Do

She might be the one who boosts you up
But frankly that's in the hands of Lady Luck
She could be your mentor
She could just as easily be your tormentor
We're told from an early age girls are made of sugar and spice
And of course everything nice
I'm not sure that the neglected souls we see
Would entirely agree
There's something amiss
When it's a mother, never again will they want to kiss
Harm from the one meant to be your protector
Sending you into the social service sector

I Seen Him Regular

Down by the pool
He never smiles not once
Except to his little girl
Then he had the look of a nonce
My wife commented
Look at him in the water
That's no way to hold your daughter
Poolside you see some sights
I'd like to take away his breathing rights

If You Want A Positive Outcome

For these children damaged
For all our futures
For generations to come
There isn't a price
There isn't a sum
For these poor souls
For their children
For the lives lost
There can't be a price
Whatever the cost

Fostering Thoughts

You foster to give
You foster to live
You foster for reward
You feel like a fraud
You get drained of emotion
You get no promotion
You get tired beyond belief
You feel guilt asking for relief
You suffer trauma
You suffer secondary trauma

Food For Thought

I could murder a steak
Meat
Deadend
choose Love
she's back
Walk Away A Winner

I Could Murder A Steak

Animals in Zoo's
For you to peruse
Calves in crates
For you to masticate
Fish dead in the sea
Full of mercury
Foxes Badgers & Deer caught
All in the name of sport
Can you comprehend their pain
Before the end
Or do you even care?

Meat

As you read this
Writhe in guilt
You are party
To the blood that's spilt
Murder in the name
Of one and the same
Question your need
For the bloodthirst you feed

Deadend

As you gorge on that flesh
Can you bear to imagine the fear
Induced into that previously healthy living creature
Does it taste so succulent when you think of the animal with its life source draining away
Is your conscience clear when you pretend it had a full and happy life
Instead of the reality
Adrenaline pumping through it's body
It's eyes bolt
As it smells the stench of death
In the sweaty surrounds of the slaughterhouse

Choose Love

Watching and listening to the man that lost his son to knife crime
Incredible composure a victim of societies most destructive paradigm
From this man who's heart was broken
Talk of Love were the only words spoken
The facts are a choice to be made
Between Love and fear
Would you rather be afraid?

She's Back

She strolled through the door
In quite an elegant way
Almost as if she never went away
The look she gave was of a superior nature
As if she were beyond questioning
And who was I to argue
So I took her in my arms to show I loved her
In return she purred and rumbled to show she loved me
Or was it the pilchards she had for her tea

Walk Away A Winner

Accidents and incidents
Actions and reactions
Talk it down
And walk away
Save your pride
For another day....

P.O.V

Anyone can Tattoo
Tatts the difference
Believe me when I say
Who voted for this ?
Why
Trauma "tis Ed
Yo
Change
Alcohol
Self Imaging

Anyone Can Tattoo

Essentially it's true
Anyone can Tattoo
A slice or prick to the skin
Then send your ink within
The outcome is what'll vary
From an image quite blurry
To something iconic
But the response you get
Could still be vitriolic.

Tatts the Difference

I'm an advocate of the Tattoo
I have one where I wear my shoe
I have a couple on my arm
They shouldn't cause you alarm
Your view of me shouldn't worsen
I'm still the same person
Your view may be clouded by stereotype
By someone you already didn't like
The only difference between me and You
.....Tattoo

Believe Me When I Say

Believe me when I say
You'll Know one day
Regardless of what you've said
It'll be different when your parents found dead ,
Ideas you had of how you'll cope
Are worth as much as a bit of old rope,
It's life and inevitable you say
Until your parents found dead one day
Then you'll know how different it is being left alone like an adult orphan.

Who Voted for This

A care system
That doesn't care
Policing
That don't police
Hospitals
They can't Hospitalize
It's all going on
In front of our eyes
So what will you do
When the need for them
Comes to you?

Why

You'll try and find some logic
For your time on earth
There is no logic
When babies can die at birth
When peace loving people
Get bombed in their homes
We're all kept updated
By videos from phones
We watch on as atrocities happen
We all feel helpless
And NATOs lines slacken
Air raids a daily occurrence
To the worlds abhorrence

Trauma 'tis Ed

Undiagnosed as a young one
I was bleached with ADHD
Regular tests found IQ of 121
I couldn't bear it though
It wasn't any fun
My brain always on the go
No peace to be found
I often thought it'd be nice
6 foot under the ground
......Quiet at last.

Yo

I was reckless and feckless
I didn't give a damn
To who you thought I was
Or who I really am
It cost me dearly love
Of family and friends
A self destructive path
But hopefully I've made amends
No one could dig me out of that pit
That swallowed me up
And made me feel like shit
I've been around the block
I've been a bit of a cock
But with fortitude I moved on
And mistakes can make you strong
So take it from me
If life's not going well
It's not necessarily how it'll always be .

Change

I'm not alone in being alone
But this piece of information
Is of little consolation
When I come to recall
How you lifted me up
Just to watch me fall
When to you my heathen soul was sold
For a seeming eternity
How could I imagine it would last forever
Like the Summer you never want to end
It was inevitable and saddening
A different kind of beauty around the corner
To restore my faith in human nature

Alcohol

I tested my intoxication
By means of a crossword
Quite apt really
As she says they're all I have
Answers flowed one after another
As they normally do on the quickie
When I was stumped
It didn't bother me
I just took another drink
Sobriety is an overrated state

Self Imagining

I'm going through this process
Trying to build a closeness
So you might understand
What it is that makes the man
Because life's trips and falls that impact
Can cause you to come across abstract
Not that you're aware
You just wonder why people stop and stare
In the end you take it in your stride
Even when those you love deride
I know Could be a bit of an arse
That was in the past
I blame it on A.D.D
Ironic because it added nothing to me
Erratic behaviour at times
A lot of things that probably shouldn't
Make it into rhymes
A fucked up beginning
That nearly had no middle
Life couldn't be more confusing
If it were a well thought out riddle

7 Up

SET UP
LEAD ON
Now we're all grown up
Biological defects
Writer
A call
Peace of my mind

Set Up

I was made to go get the ball
The one that disappeared behind the sports hall
Naive and below my years
I didn't realise I was set up by my peers
A little runt tried to start a fight
But that wasn't me I wouldn't bite
So the angry bully came from out of the shade
I recognised then the mistake I made
I remember then I was very shy
But couldn't help repeating WHY Why why ?
The fact I wouldn't engage
Just brought on more of a rage
Pinned to the ground stays with me to this day
As I saw all my "friends " pass by the way .

Lead On

So that left me so terrified
That I would carry a knife
Not with a thought to hurt anyone
But to protect my own life
Little did I know
How that scenario would go
When faced with the next bully
It's then that I realised
I hadn't thought it through fully
The type of arsehole who starts a fight
Doesn't give a fuck who's hurt in the dead of night

Now We're All Grown Up

Fast forward from the terror
The bullies Friend is a foster Carer
The bully is a Taxi driver
The bullies accomplice he's a skiver
The friend a thief lives down under
The best friend I'm left to wonder
Depend on yourself

Biological Defects

We're all damaged
Just by different degrees
Mines such an oblique angle
I only want to please

Writer

I'm a writer
Because I write
I have no control of when,
Maybe the middle of the night
Anytime it might take a hold
I grab a pen
I let it unfold
Not knowing exactly what I'll say
Enjoying the process
At the end of the day
....Or maybe the beginning

A Call

It's taken me a lifetime
To realise my love of rhyme
With words to paint a picture
Emotions I depicture
To give an idea
Of the world I fear
I vocalise using the pen
Once in black and white
To be heard again and again
And I now realise
That Offloading is my prize

Peace of My Mind

Make a present of the present to yourself
For your mental health
Don't climb the walls worrying about the future
And what it might do to ya
The here and now is the place to be
Anything else we can't foresee
So be good to yourself
For your mental health
Take time out and settle your mind
Be good to others
And to yourself remember to be kind

Certifiably Sad

Tablet Time

It was just prior to tablet time
When he let out the yell
"I'm being beaten up!"
Lying Bastard you fell!
I didn't see a thing was the cry that went up
Son of a bitch
You broke my cup
Well I'll be fucked if you're getting away with this
With that promptly he was given a Scottish kiss
It's time out for you sunshine
You've wound up too many
In too short a time
Dragged away down the stairwell
His feet dropping in rhyme

Lost Soul

I'm smoking more than ever
Whilst trying to get myself together
It's a matter of trial and error
Trying to face the terror
The terror everyday life brings to me
Even within these walls of sanctuary
I'm trying to find my inner peace
And a way for this tension to release
The answer lies from within
It's just knowing where to begin
Recounting events is a living nightmare
But they replay without my being aware
Down to every intricate detail
With no avail

Stalled

Why you looking so upset
Are you not over it yet
Pull yourself together
Things will get better
This isn't how you'll always feel
In time things will heal
You are worrying about things you can't change
Things you can't rectify or rearrange
These are the things that people say
Like tomorrow's another day
These things don't help in your head
Infact they can contribute to you wishing you were dead

Sanctuary

I'm in here for rest and relaxation
To sort out my head
We can only give you pills the rest is up to you
That's what the Doctor said
The time disappears between time for medication and meals
And in between nothing seems to heal
A witness to outbursts of violence
Hysteria and noise
And that's just the staff.

Robbed

Abused as a child apparently they say
Just didn't turn in for work one day
Such an important day one of recognition
Reprimand of a Railway Technician
It should be noted because it's quite a big clue
When he was found his lips were a misty blue
You'll never do it he had recalled someone said
I wonder did that contribute to the body found dead
A colleague had taken a call
He just encouraged him to take the fall
That lifeline the phone was lying under the feet
Of the cold tortured body that would no longer beat
Emergency Services' called in a surreal kind of way
Quite mild for the time of year an Ambulance man would say
He looks quite pale hanging from that chain

I wouldn't have imagined a dog lead could take the strain

I guess that's the way professionals cope

The way they manage to hang on to hope

If that's maybe possibly true

Should I a joke instead be telling you

The one about the man on the National Health

Whose body parts are lying on a shelf

Ready for a guy in a private clinic

But then wouldn't you just call me a cynic

Is it Just Me?

Lying in State

I've seen them on the TV
And never in a million years
Can I imagine it'd be me
Queuing 20 hours or more
I can't help but wonder
Are these people so giving to the poor
Those people paying their respects
Would they be so giving
To those society neglects
It's a strange old world
Of which we all partake
Yet some we're happy to forsake
The people who struggle the most to live
Are often the ones with most to give
Ex servicemen homeless on the street
Teachers worrying about turning on the heat
Social workers at food banks
So their children have enough to eat.

Seeds of Love

A bunch of blooms
An action I don't understand
The cutting off in their prime
It seems rather bland
Why would you for your love flowers buy
Just so they can watch them wilt
And eventually die
Instead give a plant or seeds to sow
So like your love they can nurture
And watch it grow.

Trust

To test their trust I tell a story
A story as such might not be true
Just some words to test my trust in you
No compassion or care from the guy
Just the threat of an outcry
One to sell you down the river
The fact I trusted makes me shiver
A pious prick
Full of rhetoric
Be careful how you choose your friends

Caller Number Two

So the BP boss says they have more cash than they know what to do with

Anne thinks suicide is her only way out

Society that cares seems to me to be a myth

Oil company with near 10 billion profit

You telling me they couldn't make life easier

Come off it .

People Eh!

It fucks with my head conversations you hear
Peoples priorities loudly spoken
For everyone's ear
It fucks with my head that they just don't care
They swear at their kids and push them about
Heavy handed words and the odd sly clout
The child that receives it Will probably dish it out
There's someone that's as important as interplanetary dust
There might be a friend who you should never trust
There might be a friend who's friendship never ends
There's another that'll never make amends
There'll be a stranger who'll be more forgiving
You'll often miss the dead more than the living .

NHS

Neglected by the NHS
Not a new situation
But it became more common with the Eton mess
People told to go out and clap
At a time when it's struggling
And generally the public fell for this crap
An ailing institution effectively underfunded since 2010
Rises in the amounts given well under inflation
Tories stitch us up yet again
So like workers wages they're covert cuts
That don't go unnoticed
Keep voting these wankers in You must be nuts.

BJ

Capitalists
In the Capital
The Eton Mess
He couldn’t care less
About the lower classes
And the dissent of the masses
They will just laugh in your face
Him and his mates an utter disgrace

Tóraidhe

Miss Trust
Following in the footsteps of the Eton mess
Trickle down economics
It doesn't exist
It's a political quip
That's the Tories taking the piss
Make the rich more wealthy
It's just not healthy
They'll never have enough
But the needy would be buying stuff
Assume the rich will spend that money
That's making an Ass out of U & Me
They're piling up their cash
Give it to those in need
They'll spend it in a flash
That's what'll get it moving
You'll see the economy improving
Johnson's left his mark
Taking 2.3 million from oligarchs
What will you be remembered for
Making the poor more poor?

WHy Me?

I wind people up with ease
Almost as if it's a flare
For the most part though
I'm totally unaware
Some might say I have one of those faces you'd like to hit
Frankly my dear I don't give a shit

Don’t Let The Man Get You Down

Rest and reset

Hydrogen

Miss-Disenfranchised

Another Life

Reflection

Too much information

Mental Health Centred

Loss

Rest and reset

Sometimes the simplest answers are the ones that's best
Like the one switching off your phone to give it a rest
Well Politically it's the same don't you think?
That maybe it's time for a complete rethink
The people in power should understand
Understand the working man
The reason why so many are driven to suicide
The storms of life that some just cannot ride
Surely more of even keel there should be
A little comfort for those on the lower branches of the tree
A total imbalance between those who their finances don't have to juggle
To those people with the cost of living have an everyday struggle?
The disabled disadvantaged and displaced

All deserve more than the adversity they've faced
We don't get to choose what we're born into
Your social mobility can be curtailed however much you pursue
A change That they really don't want to face
It keeps aristocracy going
And keeps us plebs in our place
We have a Class ceiling which goes on without mention
That's the Tóraidhe convention
That those in power wouldn't want to change
A system and culture to never rearrange
The only possible way to get the masses what they want
Is proportional representation to stop the powers that be being so nonchalant.

Hydrogen

Hydrogen is the answer it has to be the way
I watched a program about it
Here's what the engineer had to say
It's not so difficult to convert the cars
So why not just keep our petrol and diesel jam jars
And just have water out of our exhaust
Wouldn't that be worth the cost?
A minister on TV said she renewed her boiler
With one that could convert to hydrogen shouldn't we all be following her
The answers there staring you in the face
Upcycle what we have rather than replace
We need intelligence on our side
Rather than money makers out to deride
1.5 Billion Motors already exist
They just need converting to use this!

Miss-Disenfranchised

She goes shopping for clothes with a freezer bag
There's a clue as she walks away
Her jeans have a hole from a security tag
She has a casual demeanour
As if nothing could hurt her
As the damage is already done
A lack of attachment
She's only seeking out fun
A distraction from the busy mind
Overflowing with chaos
Drawn to her own kind
Seen as Streetwise a phrase that's a misnomer
You'd only see how vulnerable if you got to know her

Another Life

I, we, wish there was something anything that could be said or done to take away the pain but we know all too well that feeling of loss something missing, feeling like you're going insane, at these times when you can feel oh so alone and you plummet into the depths of despair, if you could just remember, though we may not always show it, we your friends, family, really do care.

No one can imagine what another person may feel, each individual has to deal with what's going on inside and how you do may be to kick out and scream , whatever you do there's nothing to hide , because emotions are natural and a sign of life , all the time you are feeling them you know you are alive, though you may not want to be there has to be hope for the future and in time you will see the little soul you longed for with open arms they'll be.

Reflection

In the dim and distant past
I'm a stranger to myself
A lost and lonely soul
Struggling for my mental health
Nobody knows what you go though
On your untrodden path
Desperately trying to find a way
It feels forbidden to laugh
To find an equilibrium
Is what I needed to do
To sanctify my soul
Refresh and renew

Too much information

The Bermuda Triangle is a result of eruptions of methane gas
The Government in power does not represent the mass
3 percent of young offenders are responsible for 25 percent of crime
Mysteries aren't mysteries given time
They want to see if there's life on Mars
Yet couldn't deliver my baby on time
Time will heal people say
Bollocks to that how do I get through today

Mental Health Centred

Should I be here
Am I amongst my own
With all these people around me
How am I still so alone
From the screams of forced medication
I retire to the sanctuary of 30 minutes meditation
Just enough time to relax and forget the surroundings
Then it's back to the real world of trepidation
Everyone and his brother tells me it's in my control
But I just feel like I've lost forever my soul
My being wanting and yearning are all gone
With the loss of my Baby son.

Loss

Made from love between us
I watched and felt you grow
Talked to you when I felt good
Talked to you when I was low
We wanted and needed you so much
But your limp and lifeless body
Was all that we could touch
Your beauty so immense
Your spirit touched my very soul
You'll live with us forever
Will I ever feel whole...

Loss
Will
Never
Leave
You

The Dying Groans of

LEVI AMES,

Who was Executed at BOSTON, the 21st of *October*, 1773,

for BURGLARY.

I.

YE youth! who throng this fatal plain,
And croud th' accursed Tree:
O! shun the paths that lead to shame,
Nor fall like wretched me.

II.

On the dark confines of the Grave,
With trembling haste I tread;
No Eye to chear, no Hand to save,
I'm hurri'd to the dead.

III.

Justice forbids a longer Day,
My dying Hour is come,
When my poor Soul must haste away,
To her Eternal home.

IV.

Methinks I see your pitying Tears,
You mourn my wretched State;
To shun my Crimes, avoid the Snares,
If you would shun my Fate.

V.

Tho' young in Years, I'm old in Crimes,
To lawless Rapine bred;
The Scourge and Scandal of these Crimes,
When living and when dead.

VI.

Is there a Man thro'out this Throng,
To sinful Robbery prone?
Forbear to do thy Neighbour wrong,
And mourn the Crimes You've done.

VII.

See angry Justice shakes her rod,
And points to Guilt's black scroll;
The terrors of a frowning God,
Distract my sinking Soul.

VIII.

Unless kind Mercy interpose,
And deep Repentance rain,
To change these momentary Throws,
For Hell's Eternal pain.

IX.

O! for a beam of Love divine,
To chear this gloomy Day;
To make me chearfully resign,
To give my Life away.

X.

Thou who did'st suffer Death and Shame,
Such Rebels to restore:
O! for thy great and glorious Name,
Accept one Rebel more.

XI.

Inspir'd by thee, I fix my Trust,
On thine atoning Blood,
To join th' Assembly of the Just,
And praise my Saviour GOD.

XII.

Farewell to Earth, farewell to Sin,
One Pang will set me free;
Support me, O! thou Rock divine,
And snatch my Soul to Thee.

Ingram Content Group UK Ltd.
Milton Keynes UK
UKHW011454220523
422143UK00001B/9